FAVOURITE FILM SONGS

THE BARE NECESSITIES THE JUNGLE BOOK 4

THE BEST DAY EVER THE SPONGEBOB SQUAREPANTS MOVIE . . 3

BEYOND THE SEA FINDING NEMO 6

BOOGIE WONDERLAND HAPPY FEET 8

CAN I HAVE THIS DANCE
HIGH SCHOOL MUSICAL 3: SENIOR YEAR 10

CAR WASH SHARK TALE 12

COPACABANA (AT THE COPA)
MADAGASCAR: ESCAPE 2 AFRICA 14

DON'T WORRY, BE HAPPY FLUSHED AWAY 32

FOOD, GLORIOUS FOOD OLIVER 16

I'M A BELIEVER SHREK 18

KUNG FU FIGHTING KUNG FU PANDA 20

OOMPA LOOMPA
WILLY WONKA AND THE CHOCOLATE FACTORY 22

ORDINARY MIRACLE CHARLOTTE'S WEB 24

SOMEWHERE OUT THERE AN AMERICAN TAIL 26

THAT'S HOW YOU KNOW ENCHANTED 28

YOU'VE GOT A FRIEND IN ME TOY STORY 30

WISE PUBLICATIONS
PART OF THE MUSIC SALES GROUP
LONDON / NEW YORK / PARIS / SYDNEY / COPENHAGEN / BERLIN / MADRID / HONG KONG / TOKYO

DOWNLOAD TO YOUR COMPUTER A SET OF
PIANO ACCOMPANIMENTS FOR THIS EDITION
(TO BE PLAYED BY A TEACHER/PARENT/FRIEND).
VISIT: WWW.HYBRIDPUBLICATIONS.COM
REGISTRATION IS FREE AND EASY.
YOUR REGISTRATION CODE IS KF134

ALSO AVAILABLE IN THE REALLY EASY SERIES...

REALLY EASY FLUTE MUSICALS
ORDER NO. AM998437

REALLY EASY CLARINET MUSICALS
ORDER NO. AM998448

REALLY EASY SAXOPHONE MUSICALS
ORDER NO. AM998459

REALLY EASY CLARINET FILM SONGS
ORDER NO. AM998492

REALLY EASY SAXOPHONE FILM SONGS
ORDER NO. AM998503

ALL TITLES CONTAIN BACKGROUND NOTES FOR EACH SONG PLUS
PLAYING TIPS AND HINTS.

PUBLISHED BY
WISE PUBLICATIONS
14-15 BERNERS STREET, LONDON, W1T 3LJ, UK.

EXCLUSIVE DISTRIBUTORS:
MUSIC SALES LIMITED
DISTRIBUTION CENTRE, NEWMARKET ROAD, BURY ST EDMUNDS,
SUFFOLK, IP33 3YB, UK.
MUSIC SALES PTY LIMITED
20 RESOLUTION DRIVE, CARINGBAH, NSW 2229, AUSTRALIA.

ORDER NO. AM998481
ISBN 978-1-84938-222-9
THIS BOOK © COPYRIGHT 2010 BY WISE PUBLICATIONS,
A DIVISION OF MUSIC SALES LIMITED.

EDITED BY OLIVER MILLER.
MUSIC ARRANGED BY PAUL HONEY.
MUSIC PROCESSED BY PAUL EWERS MUSIC DESIGN.

BACKING TRACKS:
HOWARD MCGILL - FLUTE
PAUL HONEY - PIANO

PRINTED IN THE EU.

YOUR GUARANTEE OF QUALITY
AS PUBLISHERS, WE STRIVE TO PRODUCE EVERY BOOK TO THE HIGHEST
COMMERCIAL STANDARDS. THE MUSIC HAS BEEN FRESHLY ENGRAVED AND
THE BOOK HAS BEEN CAREFULLY DESIGNED TO MINIMISE AWKWARD PAGE
TURNS AND TO MAKE PLAYING FROM IT A REAL PLEASURE.
PARTICULAR CARE HAS BEEN GIVEN TO SPECIFYING ACID-FREE, NEUTRAL-
SIZED PAPER MADE FROM PULPS WHICH HAVE NOT BEEN ELEMENTAL
CHLORINE BLEACHED. THIS PULP IS FROM FARMED SUSTAINABLE FORESTS
AND WAS PRODUCED WITH SPECIAL REGARD FOR THE ENVIRONMENT.
THROUGHOUT, THE PRINTING AND BINDING HAVE BEEN PLANNED TO
ENSURE A STURDY, ATTRACTIVE PUBLICATION WHICH SHOULD GIVE YEARS
OF ENJOYMENT. IF YOUR COPY FAILS TO MEET OUR HIGH STANDARDS,
PLEASE INFORM US AND WE WILL GLADLY REPLACE IT.

WWW.MUSICSALES.COM

CD TRACKLISTING

1 THE SPONGEBOB SQUAREPANTS MOVIE
(THE BEST DAY EVER)
(KENNY/PALEY)
SONY/ATV MUSIC PUBLISHING (UK) LIMITED.

2 THE BARE NECESSITIES
(GILKYSON)
WARNER/CHAPPELL ARTEMIS MUSIC LIMITED

3 BEYOND THE SEA
(LAWRENCE/TREN ET)
EDITIONS RAOUL BRETON, FRANCE

4 BOOGIE WONDERLAND
(LIND/WILLIS)
UNIVERSAL MUSIC PUBLISHING LIMITED/
THE INTERNATIONAL MUSIC NETWORK LIMITED/
EMI SONGS LIMITED

5 CAN I HAVE THIS DANCE
(ANDERS/HASSMAN)
WARNER/CHAPPELL ARTEMIS MUSIC LIMITED

6 CAR WASH
(WHITFIELD)
UNIVERSAL/MCA MUSIC LIMITED.

7 COPACABANA (AT THE COPA)
(MANILOW/FELDMAN/SUSSMAN)
UNIVERSAL MUSIC PUBLISHING INTERNATIONAL
LIMITED.

8 FOOD, GLORIOUS FOOD
(BART)
LAKEVIEW MUSIC PUBLISHING COMPANY LIMITED.

9 I'M A BELIEVER
(DIAMOND)
SONY/ATV MUSIC PUBLISHING (UK) LIMITED/
SCREEN GEMS-EMI MUSIC LIMITED

10 KUNG FU FIGHTING
(DOUGLAS)
BUCKS MUSIC LIMITED.

11 OOMPA LOOMPA
(BRICUSSE/NEWLEY)
IMAGEM SONGS LIMITED.

12 ORDINARY MIRACLE
(FROM 'CHARLOTTE'S WEB')
(BALLARD/STEWART)
UNIVERSAL/MCA MUSIC LIMITED/
UNIVERSAL MUSIC PUBLISHING MGB LIMITED/
SONY/ATV HARMONY (UK) LIMITED

13 SOMEWHERE OUT THERE
(HORNER/MANN/WEIL)
UNIVERSAL/MCA MUSIC LIMITED.

14 THAT'S HOW YOU KNOW
(FROM 'ENCHANTED')
(SCHWARTZ/MENKEN)
WARNER/CHAPPELL ARTEMIS MUSIC LIMITED

15 YOU'VE GOT A FRIEND IN ME
(NEWMAN)
WARNER/CHAPPELL ARTEMIS MUSIC LIMITED

16 DON'T WORRY, BE HAPPY
(MCFERRIN)
UNIVERSAL MUSIC PUBLISHING MGB LIMITED.

The Best Day Ever

Music by Tom Kenny & Andy Paley

This animated movie is based on Nickelodeon's TV series which features the adventures of SpongeBob and his various friends in Bikini Bottom, an underwater city. Its creator, Stephen Hillenburg, had his initial ideas whilst teaching and studying marine biology, before leaving to fulfil his dreams of becoming an animator.

Hints & Tips: From bar 19 onwards take good breaths and keep the slurred minims legato (smooth). Control the top C (bars 22, 26, 30 and 34), by not blasting out the air. Practise the C to get it in tune.

The Bare Necessities

Music by Terry Gilkyson

The Sherman Brothers were enlisted to completely rewrite the music for this animated feature, based on the book of the same name by Rudyard Kipling. Composed by long-time Disney collaborator Terry Gilkyson and sung by characters Baloo and Mowgli, this song was the only track to survive from the earlier, rejected draft.

Hints & Tips: Practise the change between second octave C and D in bars 6–7. This is a particularly tricky area, changing from C, consisting of one finger, to D, which is almost all fingers, creating instability.

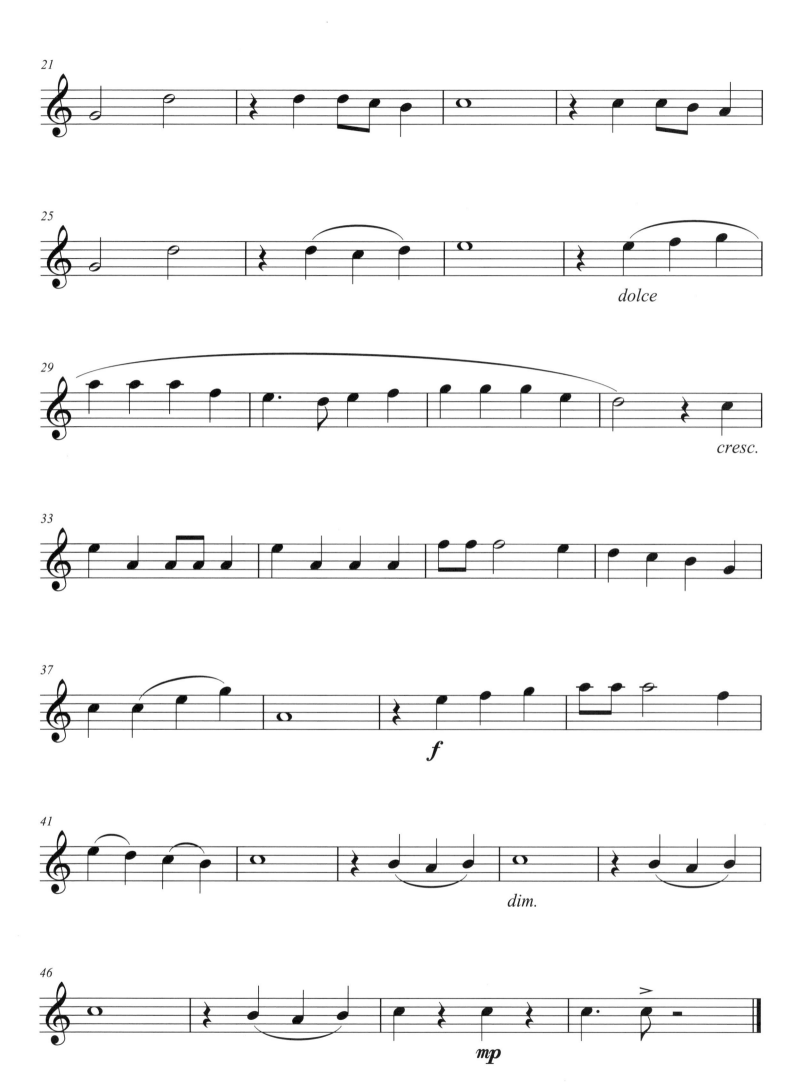

Beyond The Sea
Words by Charles Trenet • Music by Charles Trenet & Albert Lasry

'La Mer' was originally a 1946 hit for Charles Trenet and his rendition can be heard in the Steve Martin movie *L.A. Story*. In the early 60s Bobby Darin had a hit with this English lyric version (renamed 'Beyond The Sea') and Robbie Williams reprised it for *Finding Nemo*.

Hints & Tips: The key changes twice before reverting to the home key of F major, so practise each section separately before piecing the song together.

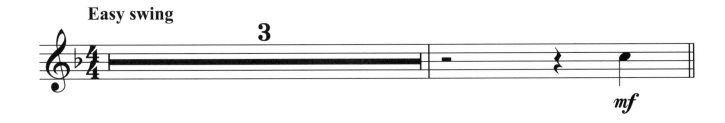

Boogie Wonderland

Words & Music by Jon Lind & Allee Willis

Unable to sing, misfit penguin Mumble has however an extraordinary talent for tap dancing, through which he eventually discovers that this 1979 disco classic by Earth, Wind & Fire is his heart song. Happy that he and Gloria can now be mates, the pair begin dancing, along with all the other penguins in chilly Antarctica.

Hints & Tips: Keep the articulation (the attack of a note, such as staccato, tenuto etc.) clear and crisp, maintaining a focussed sound.

Can I Have This Dance

Music by Adam Anders & Nikki Hassman

In this third instalment of Disney's phenomenal success, the students are coming to terms with the reality of going their separate ways after graduation. This song features twice, first as Gabriella teaches Troy the waltz and again as he convinces her to return from university to take part in the school's final musical show.

Hints & Tips: The second octave E is a difficult note to play well because it feels different for the lips to any other on the flute. This is a good chance to practise it, from bar 33 onwards. Generally this is a deceptively tricky piece to play as it mainly revolves around C–E of the second octave, so spend time practising it, the work will be rewarding for many other pieces.

With movement

Car Wash

Words & Music by Norman Whitfield

In 1977, American soul band Rose Royce had a No.1 in the US with this disco hit which Christina Aguilera and Missy Elliott perform on the soundtrack of the 2004 animated comedy *Shark Tale* in which, to advance his own standing in the community, Oscar, a young fish, falsely claims to have killed the son of a shark mob boss.

Hints & Tips: Take care of the awkward C–D transition at bar 19. Be sure to play all the correct accidentals, which are temporary alterations in pitch, such as sharps (♯), flats (♭) and naturals (♮), those that don't appear in the key signature.

Funky

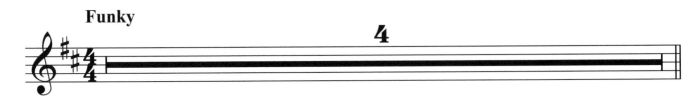

Copacabana (At The Copa)

Words & Music by Barry Manilow, Jack Feldman & Bruce Sussman

In 1978 this song became Barry Manilow's first international hit and earned him his first Grammy Award and a first gold single for a song that he composed. It tells the story of a showgirl, Lola, and her lover Tony, a bartender at the Copacabana, a famous night club in New York City named after a district of Rio de Janeiro.

Hints & Tips: Count the beats carefully before the initial flute entry. It will help to listen to the musicians on the accompanying CD. Play bars 23–25 in one breath, softly, so the air doesn't escape too fast. Take a good, full breath in preparation.

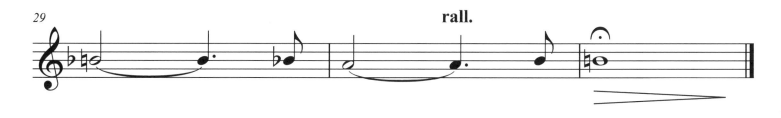

Food, Glorious Food

Words & Music by Lionel Bart

This is the opening song from the movie, based on the famous Charles Dickens novel *Oliver Twist*, and is sung by the hungry orphan boys as they fantasise about food while going to collect their dinner from the staff of the workhouse, only to be fed just gruel. Despite this, Oliver gathers up the courage to ask for more!

Hints & Tips: The music passes fast in this song and although in 2/4 (two crotchet beats in a bar), it is easier to think of one in a bar, or concentrate on the first beat of each bar. This will also help you to play the triplets evenly.

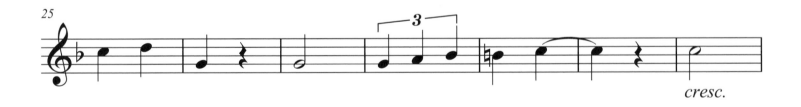

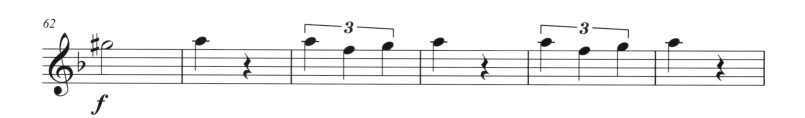

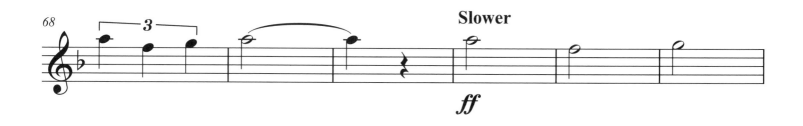

I'm A Believer

Words & Music by Neil Diamond

Awarded the first Oscar for Best Animated Feature, a category introduced in 2001, *Shrek* made notable use of pop music, including this Neil Diamond song which was a 1967 No.1 hit on both sides of the Atlantic for The Monkees. At the end, the whole cast sing it as Shrek and his bride Fiona depart on their honeymoon.

Hints & Tips: Bar 34 is marked **_ff_** (fortissimo), meaning very loud, but this doesn't mean make a nasty sound! Aim for a good, focussed sound, which will naturally be louder.

Moderately

Kung Fu Fighting

Words & Music by Carl Douglas

In 1974, at the peak of the craze for martial arts, this song was a one-hit wonder for Carl Douglas in both the UK and US. A reworked version was included in the 2008 movie, set in ancient China, in which Po, a lazy, obese panda moves from working in his family's noodle shop to fulfil his aspiration of being a kung fu master.

Hints & Tips: The rhythm is often syncopated in this song, which means the weak beats are accented, so work it out slowly before playing with the CD backing track. Practising with a metronome would be useful.

Oompa Loompa

Words & Music by Leslie Bricusse & Anthony Newley

In the 1971 film, based on a 1964 Roald Dahl novel, Charlie Bucket is fortunate to be chosen as one of five children allowed to go inside the most popular and powerful chocolate factory in the world which, because of the risk of industrial espionage, is staffed entirely by Oompa Loompas, mischievous dwarfs who love singing.

Hints & Tips: Playing the written articulation will bring this song to life; make a distinction between staccato, accents and non-articulated notes. When a piece is fast it is easy to play too loudly, but this song is mostly marked *mp* (moderately soft), so follow the dynamics.

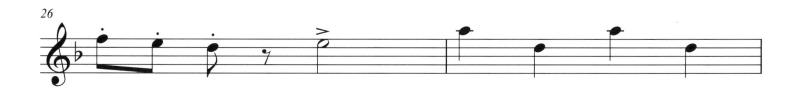

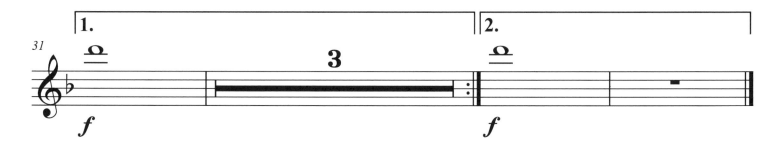

Ordinary Miracle

Words & Music by Glen Ballard & Dave Stewart

This haunting, sentimental song was recorded by Sarah McLachlan for the 2006 film, based on a novel, first published in 1952, by E. B. White in which Wilbur the pig is saved from slaughter by Charlotte, an intelligent barn spider, who writes messages praising him in her web in order to persuade the farmer to let him live.

Hints & Tips: Because of the repetitive nature of this song, once you have learned the opening phrase (bars 3–6) you will have a good grasp of the entire song. For the same reason, it could easily sound uninteresting. Combat this by following the dynamics (gradations of volume, e.g. *p*, *pp*, *f* etc.) and maybe adding some of your own. Beginning the song quietly would be a good start.

Somewhere Out There

Words & Music by James Horner, Barry Mann & Cynthia Weil

An American Tail was the first animated film made by Universal Pictures and features Fievel, a young Russian mouse, separated from his family on the way to America, a land they think is without cats. The song, which won two 1988 Grammy Awards, describes their hope of being able to see each other again.

Hints & Tips: This is a pretty melody that should be played gently, as marked. Good breath control is needed for the long phrases in bars 21–29, blowing softly and taking good breaths when possible is the key.

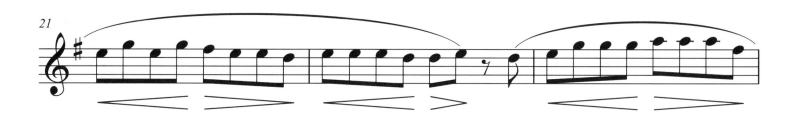

That's How You Know

Words by Stephen Schwartz • Music by Alan Menken

In a film which heralded a return by Disney to traditional animation, this song is performed by Amy Adams as Giselle, an archetypal Disney Princess, as she questions Robert, a handsome lawyer, on his views about love after finding out that he has been with his girlfriend Nancy for five years and has yet to propose to her.

Hints & Tips: There are many repeated notes in this song, play them evenly so that each is no more prominent than the next. Beware of the accidentals.

cresc.

f

mf

You've Got A Friend In Me

Words & Music by Randy Newman

Since the 1980s, Randy Newman has worked mainly as a film composer, his work on *Toy Story* establishing his trademark animation sound, subsequently carried over to several other scores for Pixar films. Nominated for an Oscar for this song, Newman finally won such an award in 2002 after no fewer than 15 unfruitful nominations.

Hints & Tips: The melody of this song quite often descends from the flute's middle to low register. Descending is one of the more difficult things to do on the flute; follow the sound with the lips by covering the tone hole with the top lip gradually, as the notes get lower. The opposite happens as notes rise.

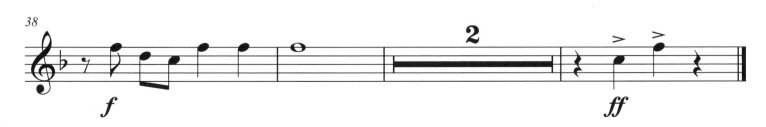

Don't Worry, Be Happy

Words & Music by Bobby McFerrin

Taking its title from a famous quote by the Indian mystic Meher Baba, this became the first *a cappella* song to reach No.1 on the Billboard Hot 100 and won a 1989 Grammy Award for Record Of The Year and Song Of The Year, although composer Bobby McFerrin never received any significant airplay for any other song!

Hints & Tips: To get an idea of how reggae sounds, listen to some reggae music, or alternatively, listen to the musicians on the accompanying CD. There are many upbeats (the note(s) preceding a melody, from the previous bar) which need to be neat and in time as it is easy to come in too late, so take breaths in good time.

Moderate Reggae feel (swung ♪'s)

123456789